MY LIFE IN YOGA PANTS

STEPHANIE HADDAD

*Melissa —
Hope you enjoy reading what's inside my weird brain... :)*

Cover design by Anna Pearlman

Copyright © 2015, 2022 E.M. Press Publishing

All rights reserved.

ISBN: 1515219534
ISBN-13: 978-1515219538

Also available from
STEPHANIE HADDAD

NOVELS
A PREVIOUS ENGAGEMENT
LOVE REGIFTED
LOVE UNLISTED
SOCIALLY AWKWARD
UNDER RENOVATION

SHORT STORIES
OTHER KINDS OF LOVE

For Belly & Buddy

TABLE OF CONTENTS

1	I am a Mom	3
2	The Mommy Uniform	6
3	Monsters in My Closet	10
4	When Size Matters	18
5	The Ballad of the Kitchen Newt	23
6	Imperfect Perfection	28
7	The Joy of Having Plans	35
8	Unspoken Words	40
9	Finding Your Moose	44
10	Writing Lessons from My Kids	49
11	The Nature of Life	57
12	Scars	63
13	A Nose by Any Other Name	68
14	I Can't Believe I Said That…	74
15	*Caffeine-Free: A short story*	77
	ABOUT THE AUTHOR	82

I AM A MOM

When you meet someone for the first time, what do you tell them about yourself? I'm assuming you tell them your name. It would be kinda rude if you skipped that part. If you're at a party, you might add how you know the host or hostess. If you're in the pick-up line at school, you might tell your new acquaintance which child is yours. If you're at the dentist, you might add that you haven't flossed since 1994.

What do you ask when you meet someone for the first time? What do you want to know about them? You might ask them what they do, where they're from, or how long they've been waiting for the bus to just get here already because it's so late that it's now early for the next pickup. Well, you might. I don't know.

But I'm not really interested in that stuff. None of those questions can tell me who you are as a person. In the interest of a good, solid introduction, I will tell you about myself. In the pages of this book, I will tell you things I would never get around to in conversation. Because the beauty of writing is that I can talk and talk and you *cannot* interrupt me. No matter how hard you try. We cannot get distracted or go off-topic, because I'm still talking.

And this is what I would say to you.

Yes, I am a mom. I am also much more.

I am a wife. I am a pet owner. I own a house and a car. I have a lot of college degrees that have resulted in a lot of college loans. I will never believe that I am done learning. I am a student and I will be for the rest of my life.

I love my children but I often see my faults in them. I also see my strengths in them and it gives me confidence that I still have those strengths within myself. I love my car but I mostly love the freedom I have because of it. The rest is just tires and metal and heated seats that are sincerely appreciated during a New England winter.

I am a writer, which you have probably figured out by now. There aren't a lot of activities I prefer to writing, which makes me kind of introverted and anti-social. When you're an introvert married to an extrovert, life can sometimes be challenging. Even so, my husband is the biggest fan I have ever had or ever will. We aren't the perfect couple, we aren't checking everything off that to-do list, and we don't have a lot saved for retirement. We do, however, have many more happy moments than sad or angry ones, and that's what really counts. We love our children and we want them to have lives as good—or better—than our own. We share the load, we cheer each other on, and we always have each other's backs.

My house is small but full of love. I don't have a

swimming pool or a private movie theater. I don't have my own office, just a kitchen table where I type away, surrounded by toy trains and broken crayons. I don't have a personal chef, a library, or half of the things that I say I "want." But I have everything I need. There is food in my kitchen, a place for everyone in my family to sleep, and a space where we can all sit and relax or play together. My house is just big enough for all of us.

I am a mom. I am a wife. I am a pet owner. I am an author, a writer, an editor, and more. I love a nice glass of wine, a quiet day of reading, and a good meal shared with family and friends. I don't like Pina coladas, getting caught in the rain, long walks on the beach, or romantic horse rides off into the sunset. I don't like hypocrisy, bigotry, or bullying. I try to be a good person every single day. Sometimes I make mistakes. I try to learn from those mistakes and move on with my life.

I am me. And I have so many more things to say.

It's nice to meet you.

THE MOMMY UNIFORM

I never meant to become part of a trend or a stereotype. I really hate those. Given the choice, I would have preferred *not* to blend into a sea of busy moms-on-the-go wearing nondescript outfits, comfortable shoes, and little makeup—if any. I would have preferred to have time for my hair instead of chopping it off, shopping for jeans that really fit instead of pulling on the same stretched-out yoga pants, and replacing those t-shirts with oil/bleach/tomato sauce stains on them.

We can't always get what we want, now can we?

It's not that I don't care what I look like or what kind of impression I give to others. It's because I don't make those things a priority.

There's a Facebook meme out there that jokes about stereotypical stay-at-home moms. *Motherhood: the only time changing out of pajama pants and into yoga pants can be considered getting dressed...* or something along those lines. I saw it and laughed, reposted it so my friends could laugh, and saw lots of "so true" types of comments. This is definitely one of those "it's funny cuz it's true" things.

A year or two ago, I met with an old high school friend and fellow mother of two. We were both dressed in black, head to toe... A weird, domestic play on the all-black-gothic-teen look of our youth, I suppose. "I see you're wearing the Mommy Uniform, too," she said on sight of me. True story.

So, what is the Mommy Uniform and what does it mean to those of us who wear it day after day? It's black yoga or athletic pants and a black top of some sort, sometimes a pop of color here or there. Occasionally, I spice things up with a t-shirt in another color, but most of mine are stained now.

Some of the "overachiever" moms often wear their jewelry and put on makeup with their uniform. Sometimes we dress it up with a nice scarf. It's comfortable, versatile, and just enough of a step above wearing sweatpants that we feel comfortable leaving the house.

What it means to us, or symbolizes to a mom, is a bit more complex. Here are some of the reasons I abide by the Mommy Uniform:

1. It's easier to track the trajectory of spit-up and other bodily fluids on black fabric. That's just science.

2. Black doesn't stain. All those bodily fluids and assorted foods will wash right out. And if it does stain, you can just use a black Sharpie to color over it.

3. Black seems professional and almost helps me to think,

"Okay, I'm off to work now!" But maybe that's leftover from my days spent working retail where black was mandatory.

4. It's comfortable enough that you can grab that unexpected nap when the opportunity presents itself. No need to change!

5. It's accommodating enough that you can grab that workout when the opportunity presents itself. No need to change!

6. It makes getting down on the floor (and back up again) a whole lot easier. There is almost never a problem with plumber's crack when you're wearing yoga pants. If you have plumber's crack in your yoga pants, you're doing it wrong.

7. Black is forgiving and hides the changes that motherhood has rained down upon our poor bodies. My hips are never too wide for my yoga pants. And I never, ever have to lay down on the bed to pull them all the way up.

8. It says, "I have more important things to do than look pretty." People take you seriously if you have a game face on.

9. There's no need for dry cleaning, thus saving you money and the hassle of running yet another errand with two kids

(or more) who need to be strapped in and out if car seats at every stop.

10. I don't really know what my pant size is anymore because my hips are in a new place. Shopping by approximated letters is easier than fitting into a number any day.

If you're not party to the Mommy Uniform and you ARE indeed a mom, good for you. I'm not saying you shouldn't care about your wardrobe and appearance. I'm just saying it's okay to reach the breaking point and put fashion aside for a little while. Or forever, whatever you gotta do. It doesn't mean you've completely fallen apart.

MONSTERS IN MY CLOSET

A few months ago, quite unexpectedly, my four-year-old daughter finally reached a stage in her life that I have been dreading since becoming a parent. She'd screamed in the middle of the night, calling out my name so loudly I was afraid she'd wake her brother. My eyes shot open at the sudden shrieking, my body turned cold. Was she in danger? I dashed from my bed, nearly tumbling to the floor in all the panic of the moment, and made it across the hallway to her room before anyone else woke up.

Elissa was standing behind her bedroom door, peering through the crack as she waited for me. At once, the door flung open and out she spilled, tumbling through the doorway and into the welcoming salvation of my arms. My eyes darted around the darkness for intruders or something that could have woken her so abruptly from sleep. There was nothing but the darkness and the nightmare that had shaken her. I stroked her hair for a moment, letting her body wrench out the last tears into the fabric of my t-shirt. Eventually her shuddering stopped and she was able to catch her breath back from the fear. Normally, this would have been my signal that the nightmare had passed and she could be returned to bed.

This time, however, Elissa looked up at me with two wide eyes and whispered words I hoped never to hear: "Mommy. Can't sleep. Too scary."

She wasn't talking about a nightmare. Although it wasn't exactly your typical "there's a monster under my bed" proclamation, I knew she meant something worse than a bad dream. My daughter has hearing loss and, as a result, a limited vocabulary based only on the experiences and objects that have impacted her so far. For her, a child who has never needed to utter a word like monster, the best way to explain the idea was just to say "scary." This was a beautiful moment for me as a mother who doubles as an unofficial speech coach out of necessity, but my joy was overshadowed by a familiar knot in my gut. I had hoped she wouldn't have to go through what I'd been through in my youth, the suffering of an overly imaginative child full of stories to tell with a head full of fictional people, places, and… creatures. All children have nightmares and, once in a while, will believe there are monsters under their beds or in their closets, but this was so much more. As much as I wanted my children to have wild imaginations, I never wanted Elissa or her brother Michael to bear the burden that came along with having one.

Unfortunately, you can't have it both ways. That night, when I asked her where the "scary" was, and then watched in horror as she pointed to her closet, I knew we might be heading down a troubling path. In that moment, as she shook ever so slightly with fear, her knuckles turning white around a fistful of my t-shirt, I would've given anything to switch places with her, even if it meant being terrified all over again, waiting for aliens to come for me.

When I was her age, my parents recognized the kinds of things that could trigger one of these imaginative episodes. After developing a debilitating fear of clowns from the movie *Poltergeist*, I found that the programs I watched on television were largely restricted. This was a smart move, even regardless of future phobias, since everything I observed became fodder for nightmares, dreams, and writings—much to my parents' dismay. I would often reuse and recycle words or plots I had seen without understanding them. I once wrote an entire short story about unicorns, each of them named by a different and particularly unpleasant swear word. My best guess is that this story was most likely the result of prime-time programming my parents watched at night, not knowing I was sitting on the staircase behind them in total silence, just absorbing it all. I was very good at sneaking back to bed unseen, my head filled with new information. After that story, however, my mother had a tough time explaining why those words weren't okay to use as names and also why I wasn't allowed to sneak around the house at night.

I got caught a few times trying to watch nighttime detective shows again. Now that they were on to me, all the fun was gone. I never wanted to disobey; I really just wasn't tired and I wanted to see what all the fuss was about these

TV shows that came on after bedtime.

As I grew older and started becoming more focused on homework and less on creative writing, Mom and Dad loosened up a little. That's when I, desperate to spend quality time with my father no matter what he was watching on TV, declared that I was old enough for a certain terrifying program: "Unsolved Mysteries." It was often a show about missing persons, wanted criminals, and other earthly occurrences that remained unexplained. Every so often, to my quick dismay, the show would feature a story about extraterrestrial beings coming to earth, abducting people, crashing their spaceships, and other types of activities a little girl doesn't want to know about. The first time this happened, I felt a powerful sensation gripping every inch of my body. It was cold, tingly, and unpleasant. I was stuck in my chair, my eyelids pasted open, and I wanted to be anywhere else. I learned much later that the feeling was terror. Pure, unadulterated terror.

The real problem, obviously, was the inevitable artist's rendering of the alien: a long, skinny humanoid-like being with a huge head and these big black, soulless eyes. Because how else would any of us know what an alien looks like if it hadn't been drawn by a sketch artist? I'd never heard of or seen anything like this before and my little brain, so full of unicorns and sunshine and fluff was ready to explode at this new knowledge. Even the detective shows had never bothered me this way. Even that terrifying *Poltergeist* clown couldn't touch these alien things. I'd heard of aliens before but despite my powerful imagination, I hadn't thought they would look like that.

I could not unseen that image. That first sighting irrevocably damaged my psyche on some level, plunging me into uncharted depths of paranoia. Still, I wasn't thwarted and forced myself to watch the show over and over, slowly scarring myself for life. All because of Robert Stack, "Unsolved Mysteries," and my own stubbornness as I swore up and down to my parents that I wouldn't get scared.

Oops.

Armed with this new knowledge of life on other planets and their unmitigated interest in abducting and studying human beings, I came to the only conclusion a nine-year-old can come to, under the circumstances: I was next. Now that I knew about their plans, they were coming for me and I wasn't going to let them take me.

My parents didn't understand my plight; they told me I was just imagining things and there were no aliens, they didn't exist. Bull! I knew they did. They should know too; they were watching the same show I was! When mom and dad threatened to stop letting me watch "Unsolved Mysteries" and thus cut off the only source of information I had on these creatures, I stopped talking about it and told them I was not scared at all. Nope, not one bit. I don't really know how I managed to convince them, but I was allowed to keep watching the show and secretly collecting my own intel.

Still in need of some help, I turned to my younger sister Samantha, who shared a room with me at the time. She helped me gather my supplies to be prepared for our alien invasion.

"Okay, what do we need, Steph?" Sam asked.

"A blunt object maybe. Something I can put under the bed and beat the aliens up with. What do you think?"

"Do you think we should have water guns too?"

"Why would we have water guns?" I asked, digging through the toy box in our room for something that qualified as a blunt object. We had a whiffle ball bat and… that was it.

"Aliens won't know they're not real guns."

"You think aliens can be killed by guns?" I asked in shock. Robert Stack would have laughed maniacally. Samantha needed to do some more research.

Admittedly, I didn't understand a lot about how to kill, or at least mostly maim, aliens. They never covered that on the show. So, she promised to help me watch and wait for these aliens every night, but I could tell that Samantha was less committed to my cause. Every night, her eyelids would droop and she'd lie down on her pillow saying she was just going to rest and boom—out for the night. Samantha was one of those kids who could have slept through her own alien abduction without even blinking her eyes, so there was no waking her. And then suddenly, I now had to stay up to protect us both. What if I dozed off and she *did* sleep through her own abduction and I could've saved her? I couldn't let that happen any more than I could let myself be abducted, so I would lie down in bed with the covers pulled up to my nose and just stare at the closet.

The closet of doom. Was it a portal between worlds

that aliens could teleport through? I watched enough *Star Trek* to know that things like that were possible. What if they came in the house when I was at school and waited for me to fall asleep so they could abduct me quietly? I mean, what kidnapper wants his victim to scream and wake up the whole neighborhood? If I could even manage a scream, that is; I was so paralyzed with fear all those nights, so many of them, that I probably couldn't have mustered enough energy to scream. I knew this in my gut, but I wasn't going to let on in case the aliens were watching me.

I spent an entire year watching and waiting for those aliens. I don't remember how much sleep I got that year, but it wasn't much. Some nights my eyes would just quit on me and I couldn't do anything to stop it. Other nights the fear was too much for my body to handle. I was gripped by it. Nothing could distract me or convince me that they weren't going to land in my front yard and break through the wall… Or teleport into my closet. It was always the closet.

Decades later, I've put the fear away and let logic step in. It's probably no surprise that I didn't become a science fiction writer, but I learned to let my imagination run free in safer areas, where there are unicorns (with appropriate, politically correct names) and lots of sunshine. The trouble is, my imagination is most likely genetic and I always hoped for my two children that they wouldn't pick up that particular gene.

Standing there, watching my little girl point toward her own closet that night, the little girl in me wanted to protect her. The adult in me knew so well that fear should never intrude on a space that is so sacred and safe as a child's bedroom. I bravely opened the door to check for aliens, something I could never do as a child. I found nothing but dresses and toys: safe, reassuring, untouched.

I brought Elissa back to bed, cradling her in my arms until she went to sleep. She was so relaxed and calm there in my arms, the love for her mommy radiating from her body. Once she was snoring lightly, I tucked her in with her favorite stuffed animal and kissed her forehead.

Turning back toward the door, the closet caught my eye again. I would conquer it this time; I wouldn't let this closet ruin her childhood. That's when I realized you can't fear what's in the closet if there is no closet.

There are most certainly no aliens or teleportation pads in my daughter's beautiful new reading nook. It's still nicely organized and holds everything she needs. Everything except her fears.

WHEN SIZE MATTERS

There's been a lot of talk lately about fat shaming, health at every size, positive body image, and the like. Plus size models are getting noticed. Obstetricians are warning about the dangers faced by overweight mothers. Fad diets are fading away as we all struggle to figure out exactly what "healthy eating" looks like. Is it cutting out fat and carbs? Eliminating sugar and gluten? Going Paleo? Or just plain watching your calories?

Am I the only one who's overwhelmed?

I've spent a lot of time thinking about my own health as an overweight woman. I've been overweight for more than a decade and, despite every fad diet invented by man, I always wind up around the same weight. Almost like it's some default setting that my body has gotten comfortable with. As a result, however, I've received quite a few lectures from medical professionals—some of which were quite insulting.

You see, the real problem is that we as a society have determined that overweight means unhealthy and skinny means healthy. This simply isn't true. As I've pointed out to my husband many times, "I'm healthier inside than most of the 'skinny' people I know!"

So, what does it really mean to be healthy? I have nice, even blood pressure; nice, even blood sugar; a good fitness level. My doctor would tell you I'm at risk for heart disease and diabetes. Yet, I've never exhibited any of the warning signs for either problem. Ever.

Shouldn't we be focusing more on what we put IN our bodies than what our bodies look like? I eat fruit and vegetables every day. I go meatless on Mondays and don't eat high-sugar, high-fat foods. I don't drink sodas or sugary juices. I get my daily water intake, walk every single day for 30 – 60 minutes, and take a multivitamin. Aren't these the things that make a person healthy? Shouldn't THIS be what doctors are asking me about?

When I was pregnant with my second child, my OB scared the ever-living daylights out of me. "Overweight mothers," she said. "Are at a higher risk for spontaneous miscarriage in their last six weeks of pregnancy. We don't really know why, but sometimes it just happens." She monitored me weekly with ultrasounds to make sure my son was still thriving, still moving around, still alive. It was absolutely terrifying to live my life in the days between those appointments.

Needless to say, we were both fine. I had a record-fast recovery from my C-section and kept the focus on nutrition and exercise during that entire time. No one could explain to me why these women miscarried. Did they have other health risks? Did they live as healthy a lifestyle as I did? Why was I treated differently because of a number on the scale? And how did the percentage of overweight women compare to regular weight women with late-pregnancy miscarriages? Taken alone, it was scary, but perhaps it would have been less so if the statistics had looked at the whole puzzle instead of just one piece. I really can't say for sure.

While I recognize that we have to use something to determine a person's health, weight cannot be the ONLY way we assess it. Someone's weight can indicate a problem, sure. But isn't it our medical professionals' responsibility to get to know a patient? If my doctor asked me for a food and activity log for one week, I bet she would be surprised. I wonder if it would make any difference. I wonder if she might finally admit that weight isn't the only way to decide if a person is healthy or not.

We're trained to assume that being "fat" means lazy, indulgent, and sloppy. And I wish I could say I wasn't also a victim of this way of thinking. As much as I rally against being classified as an unhealthy person, I have to really try hard to change my own thinking. When I meet someone who is bigger than me, what are my first reactions? I've forced myself to stop and think about this. I assume many things about that person without knowing one thing about him or her. I might assume they are lonely or depressed, upset about the way they look, unfit and unhealthy, and more. The thoughts I have are pretty awful sometimes. I'm almost embarrassed to admit it, but the conversation needs to start somewhere.

We must be able to talk about WHY we judge others by their appearance and WHAT we assume about someone before he or she speaks a word to us. Nice people come in all shapes and sizes. Healthy people can live in all kinds of bodies. I hate to say we can't judge a book by its cover because I really hate clichés, but I don't want to be judged by MY cover either. I also won't say that every person is special and unique like snowflakes. Because seriously, there are some people out there who are really terrible human beings. And I bet that most of us wouldn't be able to tell by what they look like either.

I don't have a permanent answer for how we can change our societal attitude about weight. I applaud the companies who are starting to celebrate women in all shapes and sizes in their marketing campaigns. I'm so pleased to see so many celebrities promoting a positive body image as well—they are the role models I would be happy for my daughter to have as she grows up and forms her own opinions about her body and appearance.

The changes have to start inside us, ladies (and gentlemen, because men can have body image problems too!) Before we can ask society to change its mind, we have to change our own. Learning to love myself just the way I am is a constant battle. I have to be committed to having a positive opinion of my body each and every day. Some days it's much harder than others, especially if I'm trying on outfits at rapid-fire speed just looking for that perfect thing to wear.

Breaking the cycle of negative talk about how I look is

just like breaking any bad habit. You can't really quit smoking and be cured of your cravings in one day. You can't give up sugar all at once. You can't get off the couch in the morning and run a marathon that afternoon. It takes time, training, and dedication to love yourself. You have to really want it before you can find it. You have to wake up every day and find something new to love.

Here's another cliché coming at you... You need to take baby steps. Go to the mirror right now and look at yourself. Don't squint, don't suck in your stomach, don't scowl at that mirror. Find one thing that's beautiful. Why is it beautiful? What does it show you about yourself? Do the same thing tomorrow with another beautiful part of you. Baby steps.

We all deserve love... unless you're a jerk. But if you're not a jerk and you want to change the way we are all judged for how we look, you'll have to heal the inside first.

THE BALLAD OF THE KITCHEN NEWT

Once upon a time, there were two newts who were brought home by two little girls to live as their pets. The sisters were excited to have these new pets—ones that their mother was not actually allergic to, although it was questionable whether or not these tiny domesticated lizards were carriers for salmonella. Luckily, the girls were too nervous and grossed out to handle them anyway, so this potential health hazard was never fully actualized.

In any event, the newts had a smallish aquarium to call their own. There was a rock. There was clean water. There was food. There was sunlight peeking through the windows near their little habitat. They were a pair of happy newts, marveled at day and night by two sisters who couldn't agree on what to name them. Because of this, they remained The Newts for the duration of their short lives.

Each day, The Newts watched the two girls watching them. The acrylic walls of their aquarium left nothing for privacy, but they were content with their home. The crystal-clear water allowed them to see and be seen, at least in the early days. Soon, however, the water in the tank grew murky and cloudy. The girls' eyes were on them less and less as the water grew darker and darker with their neglect.

"I told you to keep this aquarium clean," said the Mother. The Newts heard this from afar.

"I don't want to touch them!" said one of the young girls. And so, they lived, untouched and in need of help, until they could see nothing through the cloudy puddle that had once been a shimmering private pond. The girls' mother freshened their water every few days to keep things cleaner and brighter. They appreciated this immensely, but it was not enough. Eventually, the glass walls were dull and coated with dust and mildew. The walls were too high and the water level too low to give The Newts any chance of escape. The girls' indifference gave The Newts no chance of mercy. There was nothing to be done.

In time, the girls' mother lost patience with her daughters and decided to give the tank a proper cleaning on her own when they had gone to school. Her efforts, though in earnest, were to be too late to save the poor little things. So, unsure what to do with the little lizards' lifeless bodies, she placed the aquarium outdoors. There it went forgotten. The urgency the mother had felt to help The Newts had dissipated and the tank was both out of sight and mind for several weeks.

When spring cleaning time arrived, the Mother demanded assistance in tending to the horrid aquarium and its innocent prisoners. The water was dumped into the backyard, where just one little body flopped onto the ground. Whole, healthy, and still twitching with life. The remaining Newt was finally free of his prison! He looked around, surveying the wide-open space of grass and dirt now available to him. It was everything he had ever dreamed it would be to—

Be back behind acrylic walls all over again. For, you see, the Mother was so pleased to see him alive that she promised to give him a happier—and cleaner—existence. She found an empty glass bowl that was deep enough for water and a nice sunbathing rock. Although The Newt was displeased to be back indoors, his life became much happier. Happy enough that he nearly forgot about his many days spent in a darkened, blackened pool of water outdoors, left to the cold and the wind and the rain. Now, he had clean water, food, and a place to sit and sleep all day.

The Mother claimed The Newt as her own pet, restricting her daughters to toy animal pets for the foreseeable future. She found him a spot on the wide kitchen counter, where the sun's light pooled for many hours each day. She kept his water clean. She caught houseflies and insects and dropped them into the water for him. She fed him normal meals of flaked food each day. She even talked to him while she washed dishes or cooked dinner. He had companionship, finally, and it felt wonderful to be loved.

And so, The Newt lived for many months, blissful and content in his cool, fresh water. Over time, he noticed the cabinets being emptied, the boxes being folded and packed, the procession of furniture through the kitchen and out the backdoor. He could hear the clanging metal door of the moving truck open and close, the voices of the children excited to be moving to a new home.

In time, The Newt himself was soon carried out to the car and placed gingerly in a secured spot of the car. His water sloshed gently back and forth, rocking him to sleep, and he woke only when the motion stopped, the doors opened, and the people left. Often, they returned with food of their own, but The Newt was happy to wait for his flies.

Before long, the family and The Newt were in a new place, living with new people. One looked much like The Mother who had cared for him. In fact, The Newt soon grew to know her as The Grandma. The children loved her very much and she was helpful, kind, and caring. She helped catch flies for The Newt, sometimes spiders too. Once in a while, she even talked to him. The Newt had a family now and a new place in a new kitchen, with plenty of clean water and sunshine.

One day, The Newt watched The Mother and the children leave their new home. The Grandma kissed them goodbye and promised to care for him until they were back. The Newt felt relieved that The Mother would return soon. Although he also liked The Grandma, The Mother had been the first to show him kindness and care. He spent the next few days swimming and sunbathing in peace.

On the fifth day spent alone with The Grandma, she arrived to clean his bowl. She placed him inside a plastic cup near to the sink and he could see her gently wiping the bowl and the rock clean.

"We'll get you all nice and clean," she said, smiling at him. "Some fresh warm water to relax in."

The Grandma ran the tap, holding her fingers beneath the cascading stream of water. She placed the bowl beneath the faucet until the water filled half of it. Gently, she positioned the rock in the center of the bowl. Finally, she tipped the plastic cup enough for him to step out onto his rock.

The Newt dipped a foot into the warm, tropical water. It was warmer than any water he'd swam in before. Curious, he ventured from the rock and swam a slow, deliberate lap. It felt nice, like a soft caress, and he let his eyes close slowly. The water wrapped around him like a blanket, lulling him to sleep as he floated on the surface. His heart slowed and he felt a little bit lightheaded. With his eyes closed tightly, he felt his four legs go limp.

"I changed his water," The Grandma said, talking into the receiver of the phone. "I made it nice and warm for him, but he's not moving anymore."

It was the last thing The Newt heard before he drifted off to one last cozy nap.

IMPERFECT PERFECTION

I'm a perfectionist. For a long time, I thought this was a strength of mine, something to be proud of. In recent years, when perfection is even harder to achieve, I have changed my tune. Well, mostly. While I can now admit that striving for perfection can waste time and energy, create unnecessary stress, and should probably be viewed as more of a shortcoming than a strength, I can't exactly switch it off like a light.

In fact, I'd say that my perfection is more likely wired to a dimmer switch. I can tone it down, set some mood lighting, but it's never really off. I realize this means I will blow a lightbulb before that wild light of perfection ceases to shine.

Now, this isn't to say that I'm perfect. Not by any stretch of the imagination. Rather, I keep trying to get there, as if it's possible for any human being to truly reach perfection. The corners of the bed must be tucked in at right angles. The lunches must be perfectly organized like a square of Tetris pieces. Every hair must be in place. Every shoe must be free of scuffs. Both dogs must have matching collars, leashes, ID tags.

It never ends. Really. Never.

I'm also not sure when it began, but I can clearly remember the first time I learned that perfection can actually be imperfect. It also has consequences.

I was in sixth grade, struggling to find my place as a new kid in a small class of 30 kids at a Catholic school, and going through a "chubby phase." I was eternally self-conscious about my weight, my pimples, and my perm-fried hair. It was spring and I'd almost survived the school year. The weather was warming up, the flowers were blooming, and our front yard was lush and green once more. This meant we'd started spending weekends outside again, much to my dismay. I hated being outside in the wind and the sun, subject to the attacks of various bugs, especially spiders. I would have preferred to be inside reading any day.

On one particular day, I got it into my head to search a sprawling patch of clover that had sprung up in our front yard. I don't know where the idea came from, but I knew they were lucky and I figured some luck certainly couldn't hurt. So that day, I knelt down on the ground I so loathed for its mud and bugs and I searched for a four-leaf clover.

Three leaves. Three leaves. Three. Three. The search kept me occupied for a good long while. I don't know how long I was there that day, but I wouldn't give up until I had inspected every single clover. As I neared the edge of the patch, feeling hopeful but exhausted by the monotony, I saw one. I counted them again. One, two, three, four leaves.

Four! I could barely believe my eyes.

It was beautiful, perfectly intact and vibrantly green. It was just what I needed on that windy spring day.

So, I plucked it from the ground, gently, careful to preserve its four fine leaves. I needed to show this to someone, as if it could validate that I did, indeed, have the good fortune to discover one of nature's rarities all by myself. I sprinted into the house and presented it proudly to my mom.

"I did it! I found one!"

She was impressed, but immediately cautionary. "We should find a way to keep it so it won't wilt and dry up. I've got an idea." Mom always has handy ideas.

Together, we worked to preserve my good luck in its perfect, pristine beauty. After all, what good was any luck if you let it wilt, brown, and die?

Mom found an old photo sleeve, unused and discarded from a wallet at some point. I cut one sleeve carefully from the bunch and sized down a slip of paper to fit perfectly inside. With careful fingers and some pieces of Scotch tape, I affixed the clover to the paper, slipped it into the photo sleeve, and sealed up the open side. I smoothed the tape flat so it would look professional. Like I was a trained preservationist with a broad-ranging collection of botanical wonders pressed into photo sleeves.

It was beautiful. And it was perfect.

On Monday, I brought my four-leaf clover to school, tucked into a pocket of my Trapper Keeper like a secret treasure waiting to be revealed. My sixth-grade teacher always encouraged us to share stories, items, and inspirations with the class, kind of like a spontaneous Show-and-Tell open to anyone. That day, I tiptoed up to her with an ear-to-ear grin and shyly asked for my turn to share something wonderful with the class. Mrs. Thomas smiled too, even without any idea what I had with me that day. "After lunch," she said to me, and so I waited patiently all morning and all of lunch without whispering a word to anyone. I was giddy and nervous and still so, so proud.

Finally, it was time. Mrs. Thomas announced that I had something to share. The butterflies exploded in my stomach. Getting up in front of the class was somewhat terrifying for a shy girl like me, but this was something that had to be shared. The imperative outweighed any nerves I felt that day. I stood up, slid the photo card from my folder, and walked to the front of the room.

"This weekend," I began, my voice shaking with excitement. "I found a four-leaf clover in my yard and I wanted to bring it in to show everyone." It didn't seem silly at all to pass around my preserved clover. It was protected from their fingers as they handed it from one desk to another.

It was not, however, protected from their scrutiny.

"This isn't real," said Paul, when it finally made its way to the back of the second row. He always sat back there, making people laugh and attracting my sideways glances from time to time. He had been *that boy* to me for over a year by then and I wanted him to see my clover and be excited for me. I wanted him to be impressed. No such luck.

Mrs. Thomas asked him what he meant.

"Look at it," he said, holding it up for the room to view. "It's wrapped in plastic and sealed. You bought this somewhere, didn't you?" His critical gaze cut through me. I was frozen in horror.

"No, I..." My entire brain went blank. "I made it myself."

"You made a four-leaf clover?" One critical eyebrow raised in disapproval.

"Stephanie," said Mrs. Thomas. "You can't make a clover. If you bought it, you can't pretend that you found it."

"But I did find it!" My face was hot and undoubtedly red.

"Look, she's embarrassed," Paul laughed. "She did buy it."

"No, I mean I put it in there after I found it! It was in my yard!" My voice sounded shrill, panicked.

"This is way too perfect, Steph. There's no way you made this," Paul handed it off to his neighbor and sometime partner-in-crime, Shawn. "See? Look at those edges!"

I rushed to the back of the room before I knew what I was doing. I snatched it out of Shawn's hand and pointed to the tape on the edge. "Look right here! I taped it myself."

"There's no way you did that," Paul shook his head. Shawn snorted. Mrs. Thomas cleared her throat. "It's way too perfect."

I can't remember what happened after that. My

flushing face, the flood of hot tears, and the embarrassment of his accusation were too much to handle. I know that I somehow made it back from the bathroom cool and composed, my eyes red and raw, and sat back in my seat—second from the front of the class, just like always. I kept my eyes focused sharply on the board, offering not a smile or a nod for the teacher who'd hung me out to dry as she taught us grammar, geography, and science.

Not another word was ever spoken about that four-leaf clover again, at least not among my classmates. After crying over a few pages in my diary that night, I left the world's most perfectly imperfect and utterly unlucky four-leaf clover tucked into the diary's pages. Being perfect had gotten me into trouble and it had caused one of the most horrifying embarrassments of my entire life.

Such a stupid thing to pick a fight about and such a silly injustice to be angry over. But that's how life is at 11 years old and there was no consoling me for days. Weeks, maybe.

Now that I'm adult, that story makes me laugh but there's still a dull ache somewhere in my heart. Paul was so fun-loving and always so nice. Why was he threatened by something I had made, something that looked too perfect to be real? I never worked up the nerve to tell him how I felt and we parted ways after junior high graduation; he went to one school and I went to another. I never forgot that look of hatred in his eyes when he thought I was lying.

I was never a liar. If anything, I just tried too damn hard to be liked.

Today, I'm writing this and even as I'm doing so, reliving a horrible memory, I am worried that the peanut butter stain on the back of the couch belies the cleanliness of my living room. This scratch here on my laptop screen is all I can see. The cold coffee in my mug could've tasted better. My son, just two-and-a-half at this moment, is playing happily by my side but he could really use a tissue.

Even though I still have to train myself to overlook life's imperfections, I now understand how dangerous it really is to force perfection on anyone or anything, even yourself. I don't have that four-leaf clover anymore, but I wish I had kept it. It wasn't the clover that was the problem. It was me, the shy and nervous girl who wanted to make nature's perfection look even more perfect for a silly school presentation.

The next time I find one, I'll just take a picture the way it is.

THE JOY OF HAVING PLANS

There's something almost magical about making plans, especially when you're a busy mom who doesn't get out much. Movie dates, luncheons, coffee meet-ups...they fill a schedule with joy. Well, the prospect of joy. Potentially forthcoming joy, to be exact. Yes, a full calendar can really warm the heart. After all, it means you are a popular person with demands on your time. You're a precious commodity to those who know and love you. You are worth their time as well.

Not that you need the validation, of course. It's just nice to know that you matter to somebody, right? Somebody besides the drooling toddler with a wet diaper and chocolate covered fingers, that is.

Right when you first make plans, you're fairly psyched about it. A night out with the girls, for example, can become that glowing beacon in the mist of your daily routine. Adults! Food that hasn't been dropped on the floor! Clothes that aren't covered in barf/urine/feces/spit-up/ketchup! It sounds like paradise. So, you mark your calendar and start counting down the days.

Then, suddenly, that girls' night out is mere days away. How did this happen? How could so many frantic bedtimes have passed without you noticing? Did you check with your husband about his own schedule that night? Do you need to get a babysitter? And—for the love of Pete—are there any clothes in your closet that are both suitable to wear and not in need of dry cleaning? You look down at your yoga pants, which haven't been washed in—ahem—a while. Hmmm...it's a possibility.

But now, with all these questions looming, your night out with the girls has suddenly sprouted its very own To Do List. You grit your teeth. You've got enough To Do Lists already. *You said you'd go*, you admonish yourself, *and you can't cancel on them again. That would make it six cancellations this year. You're marching your way into Bad Friend territory, girl.*

And so, you buck up and decide to be a good(ish) friend and go. You check with your husband and of course, that's Parent/Teacher night at school, and since he's a teacher, he won't be home. You knew this already, but the information escaped through one of the permanent holes in your brain. You even wrote it on the calendar so you wouldn't forget, which obviously worked out great.

Right. Time to find a babysitter. A last-minute one. Which is much like finding the Holy Grail itself.

Between school drop-off, the dry cleaner, school pick-up, soccer practice and ballet class, you spend the next 48 hours dialing every number in your Rolodex. Well, at least you would if you actually still had a Rolodex that hadn't been confiscated by your 5-year-old to set up an "office" in her bedroom. That was six months ago now.

Not that you've ever been organized enough to really use it properly. Besides, you're supposed to be using your phone to stay organized now, or something like that.

Instead of a Rolodex, you've got an intricate filing system for potential babysitters: a stack of Post-It Notes scattered throughout the kitchen. One day, you could probably just put them all in your cell phone, live the bold and daring paperless lifestyle. In fact, you could probably do that now…but who has the time?

After missing all 11 babysitting targets, you're a bit discouraged. There's always family or friends, especially when you're in a pinch. To you, though, a pinch seems more like an emergency situation…not a superfluous trip to a bar. Alcohol is not a basic human necessity. Do you really want to cash in a favor for this?

Yes, you do. But like most mothers, you hate to ask for help. It's this weird phenomenon you can't explain. Your rational brain knows it's ridiculous, and yet, there are kamikaze butterflies launching an attack on your intestines right now.

Having plans is supposed to be fun, right? What happened to all the fun? And all that potentially forthcoming joy?

Sigh. You would demand the joy, if you weren't already so tired.

It's finally the day you were looking forward to all

those weeks ago. Remember that? Those happy imaginings about what it would feel like to get a break, shake up your week with something different. It sounded like stress relief, and now it has somehow begun to induce stress.

So, your husband's out late, your oldest child forgot her lunch when she got out of the car at school, your youngest got car sick and barfed his breakfast on your brand-new sneakers, then had a meltdown in the grocery store. You finally make it to pick up your dry cleaning but they accidentally made the stain bigger and now you really, seriously have nothing to wear. You look down at your yoga pants again, the cuffs stained with Pop-Tart puke, still not washed from the last time you looked at them…nope, not even you can pull these off with a cute top. Lovely. There's no time to shop between picking up the kids, shuttling them all around and then back home for dinner. Maybe you can stop somewhere on the way if you leave right when your gracious-relative-turned-sitter arrives. But there's a huge accident on the highway and that gracious relative is stuck in five-plus miles of traffic.

After all of your efforts, you must finally concede defeat to the fates. You pick up the phone and cancel on your girlfriends—again—and you know that every word you speak sounds like an excuse. None of them have kids, not even the idea of kids, and so they can't understand how someone could be so careless. The insanity that is parenthood is lost on them.

So instead of your awesome girls' night out, you spend your Thursday bathing the kids, packing their lunches, eating the chicken nuggets they drop on the floor, and tucking them in for bed before you spot-clean the puke off your pants. Just like last night and every night before that. This time, though, you give them each an extra hug and kiss.

Making plans is exciting. Having plans is one of life's great joys. Really, it's keeping those plans that is such a bummer. Oh well, there's always next time. Tonight, a nice quiet night with your kids was just what you needed to unwind.

UNSPOKEN WORDS

All of my life has been spent in the "hearing world," the part of our culture where people can hear and speak to each other with little difficulty. This world, even in the wake of texting and emails, still relies heavily on the spoken word for communication. We stand in line to order a sandwich at the deli by speaking; we listen to others speak the news to us through the radios in our cars; we speak to our significant other over a candlelit dinner. Speaking: it's the method we most often use to share information, ideas, and feelings.

Growing up, an unknowing visual learner, I used to get laughed at for how much I spoke with my hands. I couldn't tell a story without gestures, indicate a direction without pointing, or quite get a cap on my enthusiasm unless I flailed my arms. The most often heard joke was that my Italian heritage was showing through. I knew that there was more to it than that. Words felt trapped inside my whole being and had to come out whatever way they could. Speaking, I knew then, wasn't the only way to show someone what you wanted them to know. It also, most importantly, could show them how you felt.

Fast-forward to my childbearing years, when I'm still talking enthusiastically with my hands, my daughter was born by emergency Caesarean-section with the cord wrapped around her neck five times. After battling back from a five-percent chance of survival, enduring myriad treatments and drug doses, my little girl made it home from the hospital. There was one price paid for her life: her hearing nerves had been irreparably damaged and she was left nearly deaf. We had her fitted with purple glittery hearing aids, got her started with Early Intervention services, and enrolled ourselves in as many sign language classes as we could. My husband and I have spent the last five years taking classes, watching online videos, raiding the library's stacks of books and DVDs, and advocating for our daughter to get all the services possible to help her speak as well as we do.

What a hearing-world way to look at it, no? During all this time and all this hard work, I've learned something invaluable about communication. The words we don't speak to each other are so much more powerful. When I learned to shut off the DVD and just be with my daughter, finding our own way to communicate, that's when the magic started to happen. People in the hearing world might miss these things, because we don't have to look for them. There are so many lessons that are missed.

For starters, I've learned these past years that the face I make can betray the words I speak. I can stand in front of our pantry door and say, "No! No more cookies" as many times as I like. To a hard of hearing child, the volume of the words and even the anger of them gets lost. Those things don't matter, especially if I'm distracted by something on the other side of the kitchen or I forgot to furrow my brow seriously enough. If I don't look totally committed, she's aware of the weakness.

There's also no pretending around here. As we learn how the tiniest facial expressions can change the meaning of a sign in American Sign Language, my husband and I have gotten quite adept at spotting each other's missteps. There's no pretending to be happy or pretending not to be sad; there's no anger boiling under the surface, unnoticed. The words we don't speak to each other are often heard loud and clear, just because we've trained ourselves to speak another language.

American Sign Language is its own language with its own grammar and nuance. Many hearing people make the mistake of assuming there's a direct spoken word-to-sign translation guide, but that is not the case. (That type of signing does exist, but it's something else.)

When speaking ASL, facial expressions and the enthusiasm put into every movement can create so much more than a word. Using these tactics, the sign for *quiet* can become *very quiet*, the sign for *funny* can become *very funny*. Repetition of a sign can also change its meaning, as with the word *hungry* which is repeated to convey the concept of *sexual desire*. Want to swear at them? Try taking the sign for *anus* and forcefully throwing it at them. You've just called that person an *asshole*, and you'd better be sure that you meant it. Speaking ASL means paying attention to things like this so you don't accidentally offend someone.

Sign language is an amazing way to share the communication experience and connect with other people. They speak with their whole bodies, exuding powerful emotions and ideas with the movement of their hands. It calls your attention to where every part of your body is as you talk, down to the last eyebrow or corner of your mouth. We present to each other as a canvas for words, a beautiful way to really interact as human beings.

My daughter does speak most of her words and our plan is to continue schooling her in sign language as a means to verbal communication. It's working so far; I know there's not a chance this little girl would ever stop chattering away or signing her favorite songs now that she has started. Still, here in our house, I know that the words we don't speak to one another will always ring true. My husband, daughter, and now my hearing son, will all be able to share in this most beautiful way of communicating with me. It's nice to finally have a real use for my talking hands.

FINDING YOUR MOOSE

Everyone has that one unattainable goal, that singular to-do that can never get checked off the list. For many of us, this is a generic, long-term goal that we don't have the steam power to reach—hitting that goal weight, saving your first $1 million to retire, or taking a trip around the world on the yacht you don't own yet. These are the goals we say we want more than anything, and yet so many of us just let life go by without fulfilling them. Why?

I think they're too big. The goals have become so big and so important that they are unachievable. It's like standing at the foot of Mt. Everest and thinking, "Holy mother of God. How am I going to get to the top?" But even as you have this thought, you already know that Sir Edmund Hillary climbed Mt. Everest when no one had ever done it before. I'm sure plenty of people told him it was a ridiculous idea, and yet, up he went.

I've spent a lot of time considering this, as you might be able to tell. What makes some people able to climb the mountains and others unable? Am I supposed to decide which type of person I am? And what does that look like?

Now I'm not a motivational speaker and I certainly have no business offering hiking advice, but I think I'm getting the idea. You need to be determined, to see the small goals that lead you to the big goal, and to stay positive the whole way up. One foot in front of the other, as they say. As soon as you think you can't get there, you're heading back down the mountain. It's harder to put into practice, but there it is.

So that's how we can climb mountains, people. I hope you're taking notes. But what about goals that are outside of our control? What if the fulfillment of your goal wasn't actually in your hands at all?

My mother-in-law has one of those conundrums and the goal itself is as strange as the story of how it came to be. Sure, she has a lot of goals just like everyone else—taking vacations, staying healthy, saving for retirement, and the like. But what she really wants more than any of that is just to see a moose in the wild.

I know, I know. I've seen a moose in person and I keep warning her to be careful what she wishes for. "And when I saw this moose…in captivity…I was really glad he couldn't get out!" That's what I usually say but it never sinks in. When you really want something, that's how it goes.

So why a moose? It started when my parents-in-law were dating, heading up toward the mountains for a mini-vacation. Somewhere along the way, it was suggested that she might see a moose in person. The way she usually tells this story and the wonderment of the idea, it almost sounds like she expected to stumble upon a picturesque nature scene.

I can almost see her—the younger version I've come to know from old family snapshots. She walks gently through the woods, stepping over fallen branches and rocks, the dried leaves of many autumns crunching beneath her feet. My some-day father-in-law follows behind her, with a little more trepidation about the prospect of a 10-foot-tall moose in the wild, and whispers his warnings.

"It's too dangerous. We've come too far in the woods," I imagine him hissing these words, his eyes always taking in every inch of the darkening forest. My father-in-law is not a nervous man, but he knows when it's appropriate to be on guard. He decides to try again: "Come on!"

Now, I have absolutely no idea if that actually happened. That's my writer's imagination filling in the blanks of the story. What I do know is that she didn't see a moose on that trip, or the next, or the next, or the… you get the idea. And here we are now, several decades and countless north-bound vacations later, but still no moose. It's been going on so long that it's become a family joke.

The last time we were up there, on a family trip to the gorgeous White Mountains in New Hampshire, I spotted a bus touring company that promised a moose sighting on every trip up the mountain. Maybe not every trip, but it was something like 99% of their trips. That's as close to a guarantee as you'll get when it comes to wildlife creatures, I'm sure.

I pointed it out and suggested we should give it a try.

She sighed and shook her head: "I went on that bus trip the last time I was here and I told the driver, 'With me on board, you won't see a moose.' He promised me I would…"

But no, there was no moose to be seen that day.

"I think I jinxed them," she said, shrugging her shoulders.

During that same family vacation, on the one day I spent alone, I drove the one-hour trip to the outlet shops. Peace, quiet, and so many good deals… Ahhhh, vacation. So, there I am, driving along, all on my own, passing Moose Crossing signs every mile or so. These are the signs that make my mother-in-law sit up straighter in her seat and scan the woods for antlers. For me, they are the reason I keep my foot hovered over that brake. I don't know about you, but I'm not going to be the one to kill, maim, or just piss off a giant bull moose out there in the woods by myself. Nope.

There I am, driving along, and something catches my eye. Yes, yes, it's a moose. He pokes his huge head out from the tree line, almost like he was waiting to cross, and he froze when he saw me coming. He didn't want to get hit any more than I wanted to hit him. That's okay by me. *Stay there, Mr. Moose. I'm almost out of your way.*

Just like that, I drove past a moose. A giant moose traveling out there in the wild, in his own habitat, ready to take on my SUV if need be. I hadn't asked to see that moose and I also couldn't tell my mother-in-law about it. I could just imagine her disappointed expression, especially since she had thought about coming with me to go shopping that day. If she'd been with me, she would have seen that moose.

What's the moral of my story here? Well, I suppose there are several things you can take from it. I've learned a lot watching her struggle with her unattainable goal. Number one, opportunity is everywhere and sometimes where you aren't expecting it. I know she's kept herself near to those mountains, but proximity hasn't quite been enough for her yet. Number two, staying open-minded can make a big difference. I'm not saying that she jinxed that bus trip by saying outright that she wouldn't get to see a moose, but getting defeated by a hard-to-reach goal never helped anyone reach it. Would it help if she really believed she'd see one? Maybe. I don't understand the weirdness of the universe either.

Finally, lesson number three: sometimes, life is just about dumb luck. I didn't ask to see a moose, I was just in the right place at the right time. I didn't believe I'd see one. I actually hadn't thought about seeing one at all. It was not my goal and yet, I accomplished it. Life is weird. Life is also unpredictable.

In reality though, I really hope she does get to see that moose someday. Even if it scares the living daylights out of her for a minute or two. Because I know she'll be happier to be scared in person than to never get the chance to check it off her list.

WRITING LESSONS FROM MY KIDS

I've probably been a writer since before I could read. I remember the day my mother handed me a pen and pointed me toward my first diary. And everything I've experienced throughout my entire life has helped to shape the type of writer I am today. It is this way with all of us, not just writers, as we process and digest life's curveballs, encounters, and changes. So, from the moment that tiny plus sign showed up on a pregnancy test more than six years ago, my journey into motherhood has greatly influenced how (and what) I write.

This goes far beyond the things a reader of my novels will notice on the surface. Yes, I wrote about a woman with hearing loss. Yes, I have added little anecdotes about young children into almost all of my novels. Yes, I like to play the "secret baby" card once in a while (not that I ever had a secret baby, but it is a really fun device to use.) From talking about pregnancy and labor to those day-to-day mom mundanities, I've got a front row seat that informs my writing in a whole new way.

Beyond all of those things, however, being a mother has actually helped me to write better. It has taught me lessons as a writer, not just as a person, and not just as someone searching for a plot or fictional device. These are some of the lessons my daughter and son have imparted on me in their first few years together…

Lesson 1 – A Blank Page Can't Be Edited

Toddlers are a lot like dynamite. They're small and compact and their tempers are very easy to ignite. Above all else, however, toddlers are destructive. It's just part of the territory when you're the parent of a young child—or two. It's this driving force to destroy that has caused me to learn this lesson. Sometimes, you just have to break something down completely before you can put it together properly.

For example, the average block tower takes me anywhere from five to 20 minutes to assemble, depending on how well my nearby toddler is paying attention. Once this child catches on, however, the decision is made within seconds to destroy it. The actual destruction takes even less time. My efforts wasted on a tiny wrecking ball who doesn't appreciate the symmetry of my block assembly, the structural integrity of my design. What's the point?

When I see the sheer zeal on my child's face as he obliterates my work, however, I understand why I must build the tower. Over and over again. To break it and rebuild it, the tower must first exist. And so, it is in writing. They always say you can't edit a blank page. Editing is a terrifying process of destruction, redesign, and false starts. You may find yourself deleting, rewriting, or creating new text just to make it all fit together the way it needs to.

Every time I build a new tower, I have the chance to make adjustments. One day, I might build an indestructible tower, although this is very unlikely. At least when it comes to editing that page filled with words, sentences, and paragraphs, I'll have a chance of finding a structure that actually holds up.

Lesson 2 – If You Don't Get the Answer You Want, Keep Asking…

I'm sure every parent will say this but I don't care, because I know it is absolutely true: my children are the most stubborn little people in all of creation. Stubborn and persistent, like sneezes after you've just cleaned out the attic. Nagging, repetitive, and downright annoying to deal with at times. I love my children and I recognize that persistence is a good quality to have, but man, I'd like a break.

They've taught me a valuable lesson that I have forgotten since the days of my own childhood – if mom says no, ask dad. If dad says no, ask mom again. If mom says no again… You get the idea. They ask and ask and ask. They try different ways of asking, like negotiation and bargaining. They wait until you're distracted to ask. They whine and cry and throw epic tantrums. When my children want something, they will do whatever it takes to get it.

Not that I give in—ever—and spoil my children. They

forget that their stubbornness was directly inherited from their father and me. Still, their persistence reminds me that I don't like taking no for an answer either.

So how the heck does this teach me anything about writing?

You see, writing is hard. Editing is harder. Publishing is hardest. Today's traditional publishing industry is like a fortress. Personally, I have a stack of letters that say NO, a separate stack that say MAYBE, and an empty file folder saved for one that said YES. Giving up was never an option, not until I got to realize my publishing dream, which leads me to...

Lesson 3 – And Then Do It Yourself Anyway

I know, I know. I'm cheating because I turned one lesson into two list items. But really, this second-half is a separate lesson you should learn on its own.

When my kids don't get the snack they wanted or can't find the crayons they lost in the couch, they come up with their own Plan B. This usually means teamwork, with one child spotting the other as she climbs to a higher shelf in the pantry for that box of off-limits cookies. Sometimes, it means ransacking the junk drawer and mommy's purse for a highlighter, pen, or permanent marker to practice letter-writing. They always seem to find a way to get what they want on their own. This makes time-outs necessary, but their ability to think on their feet is inspiring.

Breaking into publishing is not only difficult, but for

me, it didn't make any sense. Here I am now, writing the way I want, picking the covers that I want, and being proud of myself. I said YES to my own work and it feels good. I don't know if I would have been brave enough to do it if I didn't remember how stubborn I can be. While the reading world has slowly discovered the validity of self-published authors, small presses, and independent writers, there's still this stigma against people like me. It's a real bummer, let me tell you. But sometimes, it's the best way to get that "yes" you've been fighting for.

Lesson 4 – You Can Make It Pretty, but You Can't Make Everyone Like It

Once both of my kids were old enough to start eating "real meals" with us at the table, I fell back into that perfectionist mode I mentioned several chapters ago. They have coordinating utensils and plates, with little sections for all the different foods I offer them for breakfast, lunch, and dinner. I used to spend a few minutes arranging things nicely in these plates: corn over here, chicken here, some mashed potatoes in this section, and some mandarin oranges right over there. I made colorful plates with a variety of foods I knew they would eat. With so many options, I thought, I had a good chance of feeding two happy little children.

This is the stuff of fantasy, gentle readers. There is absolutely no such thing.

Presenting these beautiful culinary arrangements to my

children taught me our next valuable lesson: you really can't please everyone. If one child was excited about dinner, the other hated it. If the chicken looked yummy, the mandarin oranges were so insulting they needed to be fed to the dogs. If the corn touched the mashed potatoes, mealtime was now over. I can't please them both.

With my writing, I have had to accept that I can't please everyone. This was tough to swallow as I sat and read reviews online. A writer should never do this, anyway. Will one reader's impression of your work cause you to change how you write? If the answer is no, don't read the reviews. If the answer is yes, you might have to reevaluate your commitment to your craft, friend. Just saying.

Sometimes, I ask my friends to peruse those online reviews and tell me if there's anything I need to read, i.e. something positive that will make me feel like the best writer in the history of time and space. That happens once in a great while, but mostly I just keep my head down and type, type, type away. I know what I want to write. I know how I want it to look.

Just as I can't just stop trying to get my kids to eat their dinners, I cannot stop writing and sharing it with others. For me, it is one of life's imperatives. That means I'm going to have to be okay with not pleasing everyone.

Lesson 5 – Use Your Words. No, Really.

If you've ever taken a writing class in your entire life, you're familiar with the phrase "Show, Don't Tell." What does this mean? Basically, as a writer, it's your job to craft a scene that shows the reader what you want them to see, not just tell them about it. You could say, "She looked sad" and that's perfectly good telling. But it's more enjoyable to read, "The corners of her mouth fell, her eyes lowered." That's one way to show the reader that someone is sad. I'm sure there are writers who can do a better job at this, but that's enough to get the point across. I hope.

When talking to my children, I often find myself misunderstanding them. If I think my son wants to play catch but he really wants to practice kicking it instead, we're going to have a miscommunication. The phrase "Use your words" has become a somewhat comical and stereotypical parent-ism. We all know what it means. Words can be the key to understanding between two people, the difference between frustration and happiness for many toddlers.

So, it is in writing, when words can be used to paint a picture. If you don't know what you're doing, you might give a reader the wrong idea. I know I've done it, something I learned by reading those forbidden reviews I was just talking about. There is always room for improvement when it comes to my writing. There are a million ways that I could use my words more effectively. It could mean using simple, directed language. It could be stepping back to paint a full picture of a scene. It could even be zooming in for a close up on a character's sad frown and inner thoughts.

Words are powerful tools. They should be used as much, and as well, as possible.

I know that it is my job to teach my children many things, including how to build and not destroy, how to be more patient, how to be less picky eaters, and how to expand their vocabularies. Teaching and learning are a two-way street, however. I never thought two little people who can't yet read would teach me such vital lessons about writing, but here we are. I can't wait to see what else they'll teach me.

THE NATURE OF LIFE

I am a proud descendant of a long line of women with vibrantly green thumbs. My mother had a large garden that ran the length of the property of our home, filled to the brim with tomatoes, zucchini, squash, carrots, broccoli, and one year, even watermelon. She picked grapes from our own vines in the fall to make jelly. She taught me how to keep the birds out of her strawberry patches. Whenever we could go apple picking, we'd be stocked with apple pies, applesauce, and apple jelly for the year. If there's one thing I know, it's that my mother knows how to use the earth to feed her family.

Her mother, my beloved grandmother, had an even bigger garden. She used to take me out there every morning in the spring and summer. I helped her weed up and down every row, check under the leaves for ripened tomatoes or bell peppers, and even hold the basket while we harvested fresh fruit and vegetables. Her garden was twice the size of my mom's, stretching across the yard in neat, orderly rows, the dirt carefully formed into mounds to support the growing roots. Some of my earliest memories take place in that garden, surrounded by the crops my grandmother lovingly tended. I didn't appreciate that scene for what it was: the living testament of what's possible when man cares for nature. At the dinner table each night, it was clear that nature would also care for man.

My grandmother's grandmother, who I never met of course, had come from Naples, Italy. Gardening wasn't a hobby there, it was a way of life. Gardening was in my blood; it was part of my heritage. Yet, my little thumb has no hint of green at all.

As much as I was around gardens, crops, nature, and fresh produce, I never wanted the responsibility of so much as a houseplant to care for. As a teenage girl more interested in reading books cooped up in the house, my parents went to great lengths to entice me to come outdoors. I was often assigned chores like raking the leaves or the lawn clippings, horrible tasks for someone with allergies to mold and grass. Even digging in my mother's garden stirred up the mold of decomposing plant life, making me sneeze. It was miserable to be outside, much safer to sit in my favorite armchair and read. Nature hated me, so I began to loathe nature.

Living in a college dorm and then in mostly urban areas after graduation, avoiding nature was easier than ever before. When we did rent a house, it had a postage-stamp size yard that was no good for gardening anyway. One of my roommates, Jessie, was a plant expert, with a green thumb to match the color of my grandmother's, and convinced me that they were nice to have. She had them all around our apartment and I often found myself admiring them. It was so *grown up* to have houseplants, wasn't it?

"They're pretty easy to care for," she told me, once I was brave enough to express my interest. "I stick to ivy and spider plants because they're pretty hard to kill."

"So… just water them?" I couldn't deny my curiosity anymore. After all, bringing nature indoors was the best-case scenario for someone like me. "Do I feed them or something?"

"I've got a few clippings you can have. Just water them for now, but not too much," she said, smiling. Maybe she'd been waiting for me to take an interest. She had always liked to share her interests with me: quilting, knitting, 80s cartoons. We were both excited to have another topic for discussion and learning.

For the next eight years, I kept houseplants, usually ivy and spider plants. Every time I got ambitious and bought a new plant at the store, it died within days. Jessie was right about that; I needed to stick to the stuff that was harder to kill. One particularly sad potted African Violet was all the proof I should have needed, and yet I went on to massacre potted daisies, mini rose bushes, and an aloe plant before I had given up. My mother once brought me Easter lilies, which I left happily outside both because I am violently allergic to the pollen and because I thought they would thrive in the spring air. They were pretty content out there, until the frost came two nights later, freezing them in a wilted mess of leaves and petals forever. It was a very disappointing way to start my spring.

For a while, my husband and I moved around a lot. Then we had our first child. My plants were relegated to the balcony—a certain death in New England—and I never got back into the habit again. I missed the plants, but I was preoccupied just remembering to feed the baby and let the dog out, as I adjusted to life as a stay-at-home-mom. Who has time for plants?

We finally bought a house in the spring of 2012. My daughter was now two years old and I was pregnant with our second child, a son due in the fall. That summer was transitional for us in so many ways; slowly but surely we did the things that people do when they settle into one place for a while. We embraced suburban life, bought a lawn mower, made plans to fence in our yard, measured to see if we had space for a volleyball net, and hosted quite a few barbecues on the back porch.

Sitting there that summer, swollen with new life from my neck to my ankles, I squinted in the sunlight to absorb my surroundings. Finally, I had my own yard and all the possibilities it held were mine to uncover. Could we put a kiddie pool over there? Maybe we should put down some stone blocks and get a fire pit on the other side too. And here…my eyes scanned the stretch of lawn between our yard and the neighbor's…

"Maybe I should plant a garden," I said, blinking into the sun. I wasn't talking to anyone, but my husband heard me nearby.

"That's a good idea," he agreed. "You always said you wanted one. That's the perfect spot."

I did? I always wanted a garden? I thought about my life so far and all the times that nature had been my antagonist. Still, I could remember myself saying at least a dozen times that I thought it would be nice to have a garden one day. Why else was I practicing on those plants? Why else had I cached away all those memories of weeding, thinning, picking, and harvesting? One day was here now. Well, maybe not until the following spring. I was far too pregnant to even see much of the ground, much less tend to it.

I started making my plans. I called Jessie for advice. I bought planter trays at Walmart—because even the best gardeners have to stick to a budget. I stockpiled seeds and made a plan for what I wanted to grow. I could almost taste the fresh tomatoes, crisp zucchini, and savory herbs I would plant and reap. I even stocked up on allergy pills. Now, I was totally ready to begin my brand-new relationship with nature.

Unfortunately, nature wasn't quite ready for me yet. My first spring's crops included 12 green beans and seven summer squash. I made some fundamental errors, like planting things too close together, losing track of which plants were which, and not thinning the tomato plants before they overtook the entire garden. They basically crushed my bell peppers and all the herbs I planted. Then my entire garden got some kind of virus; the leaves all spotted and began to wilt. Even my humongous squash plant couldn't fight it off.

So now what? Spring is almost here once again. It's been a year since I finally found the strength and desire to rip up part of my lawn to create a garden, battling my fear of spiders and about 600 varieties of worm to do it. Although that patch of earth is still covered in snow, I can hear it taunting me.

"Go ahead, Steph, take your best shot! Let's see if you can grow something *this time*!"

I've never been a woman to back down from a challenge. I'm still hungry for those vegetables, too. I may not love nature yet, but if I have my way, we'll be learning how to take better care of each other by harvest time. Even if I only get 13 green beans, 10 summer squash, and a single tomato this year, I'm going to call it a win.

SCARS

I have an ugly scar. It's about two inches long and still bears the pattern of the 13 stitches that once stretched across it, a sick connect-the-dots that sometimes mesmerizes me. This scar sits on my forearm, just below the wrist, and pulls the skin into a twisted grin with the edges turned up toward my hand.

It is always visible to me throughout my day, located in just the right spot where it cannot be ignored. Even now, it lurks in my peripheral vision as my hands type out these words. I can see this scar when I work, when I drive, when I eat, when I wave hello to a friend, when I change a diaper, when I sign the alphabet with my children, when I zip a tiny jacket. The scar smiles at me day and night, marring the smooth, soft, pale skin connecting my hand and wrist to my forearm. This is a strong part of my body, stronger than I ever thought it could be.

The scar sits there as a reminder. A constant, silent reminder of how blessed I am.

I think it's beautiful.

If I didn't have this scar, my life might be much different than it is today. On the night that I earned this scar, I had allowed my attention to drift from my son to my daughter as she sat on the floor of my bedroom, struggling to pull on her winter boots. I turned away from him to help her, just for a moment. It always feels like it's just a moment, doesn't it? That moment could have been so mundane, so ordinary. And then it wasn't.

I felt the whoosh of air go by me and heard the clatter before I saw anything. I knew what was happening before all five senses could catch up. There was a tiny gasp of surprise and then I acted.

As I turned toward my son, I saw it all happening. He had climbed into the drawers of our bureau, which was now hurtling toward me. I looked at him as he fell toward the floor, eyes full of fear and surprise, gripping the handle of the top drawer tightly. He was terrified. My baby was terrified.

I can't explain how I stopped the dresser, not really. I can't explain what happened in that millisecond which seems like an hour of lost time when I replay the scene in my head. I've never been so scared, but instead of running away, I leaned toward the danger. I turned toward my little boy and stuck out my arm, the only shield between him and certain harm. It was enough.

In the emergency room, the staff was kind and understanding. They didn't accuse me of "letting" this happen to my child, of not paying attention, of leaving him in danger. They smiled and they tried to lighten the mood as my injuries were tended. Some of them hung on my every word as I told them the play-by-play of how it had happened.

One of the nurses even asked me how I knew what to do. "I would have been so scared! I probably would have been frozen on the spot!"

I don't remember what I told her then, but I understand it now. Motherhood isn't about thinking or logic. It's just instinct and reflexes.

So that's how I got this scar. I didn't break any bones but I suffered from some serious bone and tendon bruising, long-term nerve damage that's still vaguely present, five internal and 13 external stitches, and a round of specialty consultations and physical therapy. I'm going to recover fully, all except for the scar.

When I got home from the hospital, somewhere around four hours later, I was still in shock. In fact, the shock takes a long time to wear off, which I hadn't expected. The reality hit me like a train about 36 hours after the accident happened. I could have been seriously hurt. Like, much more seriously. And my son could have... I couldn't even think about it. But if that dresser could do what it did to my arm, I couldn't bring myself to think about what it would have done to him if I hadn't been sitting on the floor right there. This could have been a very, very different essay.

All at once I was so grateful. He has a guardian angel, of this I am sure, and this angel saw to it that I protected my little boy. I will bear this scar proudly because of this truth.

At the same time, though, I knew deep down that this never should have happened at all. That guilt hit me in the gut. This accident, this scar, was really my fault from the beginning.

I know this sounds like typical mother's guilt, but trust me, I've had that too and this feels different. It took days, possibly weeks before I could objectively think about what had happened. If the dresser had been secured to the wall. If we hadn't been in that bedroom. If I hadn't let him out of my sight. There were too many ifs, the guilt was crushing me.

And then I remembered something.

The last time I had blamed myself for something horrible, it was the traumatic birth of my daughter. She was wrapped in her umbilical cord struggling for air and when labor set it, so did her distress. The doctors acted quickly, they knew what to do, and they got her out of there. She had a very slim chance of making it after that and we stayed by her side throughout her entire recovery. For 67 days, I sat in the neonatal intensive care unit punishing myself with guilt. Why didn't I tell someone I had a bad feeling about her the day before? Why didn't I sense that something was really wrong? Why did I dance at the wedding I went to that weekend? How could I have taken for granted the health and safety of my child? The thought that I had caused this horrible problem was too much to bear.

The nurses there were amazing and not just in their ability to care for sick babies. One day, one of the staff sat next to me and put an arm around my shoulders. I cried and cried and cried. She had anticipated the hot, stinging tears and she sat with me until they were all dried up.

"You know that it's because of you that she's here, right?" She squeezed me tight as she said these words. "She is fighting for you. Every day when you come in and she hears your voice, that little heart rate there on that screen? It shoots up 10 or 15 more beats. She knows you're here and she wants to go home with you."

I couldn't change what had happened. Even if it was my fault, which it obviously wasn't, I was going to keep fighting for her to come home. During all those days there, all I kept saying was, "Why not me? Why is she sick and I'm here, walking around and living my life?" It was hard to watch her on the respirator, hooked up to machines, and held in a drug-induced sleep. I would have traded places in a heartbeat.

There. That was the moment. I couldn't trade places with her, but I did protect my son. I went to the emergency room instead of him. I had gotten my wish to be injured instead of my child, to bear their suffering, and offer them the protection that a mother can provide.

I stopped blaming myself. I don't think I'm a hero because I know that I could have prevented it. The change was inside of me, where I let myself be free of this guilt and remember that I had done my job. Accidents happen. We all make mistakes. All we can do is learn from the mistakes, let the wounds heal, and push forward.

When I see that scar now, I smile.

A NOSE BY ANY OTHER NAME

I'm not exactly sure when I first noticed it or what event could be traced back as the source of my hatred. It might have been a bad angle in the mirror, a side-profile in a snapshot, or maybe the rude comment of a classmate. Whatever the source, somewhere along the way from childhood into adolescence, I became acutely aware of my nose. *Aware* is too soft a word here. Perhaps a better choice would be *obsessed* or *horrified* or *mortified*.

From that unknown moment in time, my nose became the enemy. I often stood in the bathroom, staring at my nose reflected in the mirror. It was bigger than it ought to be, had a bump right on the bridge, and it seemed to be growing just as fast as the rest of me. There in the mirror I would stand transfixed until I was cross-eyed, tracing the downward slope of my unsightly nose over the hump and slowly down to the rounded tip. How could I ever be pretty with this monstrosity on my face? Where had it come from, anyway? What could I do to make it go away?

When puberty hit, my nose got worse and took most of

the blame for my acne. It was oily and shiny all the time, a breeding ground for dirt and bacteria. So many zits popped up on and around my nose; it was all I could do not to wear a ski mask every day to hide the mess that my skin had become. If not for my nose, I could have had perfect, clear skin like all the girls in skin with tiny noses that were never shiny. My nose was ruining my life.

In junior high, I had my first real crush on a boy. He used to tell me I was smart and talk to me at lunch—yes, even at lunch! We were made for each other, so I thought, and I spent many long days pining for him to notice that I was, indeed, a girl. His attention was almost enough for me to forget about my nose and all its problems. At least it was, until I finally worked up the nerve to approach him at a school dance.

"Hey Paul," I said, wiping sweaty palms down the sides of my brand-new dress. It was blue, his favorite color, and that had been no accident. "Do you want to dance to the next slow song?"

"Oh," he said, grimacing. He made no attempt to hide his dislike for me and my brilliant idea. I braced myself for the worst. "I actually promised Sarah I'd dance with her."

Instinctively, I glanced around behind me and there was Sarah, not even wearing a blue dress, but with her perfect little round nose and no greasy T-zone or pimples. She was talking to her best friend, the second most popular girl in our class, and they were laughing away.

Laughing, I was convinced, at me and my stupid nose.

That day was transforming for me, serving as a constant

reminder that someone like me could not be loved. Not with this horrible, awful nose planted square in the middle of my face.

High school came and I attended a prestigious all-girls' school where I didn't have to worry about boys or looking pretty every day. Sarah and her best friend Courtney also attended this school, but I noticed they weren't too preoccupied with their appearances either. They never had a single pimple that I saw, but at least their hair was messy once in a while. I embraced the boy-free culture and stopped worrying about my nose for a time. Yet, class pictures and yearbooks, home snapshots and videos, and even that stupid bathroom mirror would creep up and remind me of the sad truth. There really was no escaping my nose.

I met my husband during those high school years and, even as a young man, he never looked at my face with disdain. He never said a word about my nose and never rejected me because of something silly like my looks. When I was with him, my nose wasn't a problem anymore. I was learning to live with it instead of fighting it, which basically meant that I wouldn't look directly at my nose. I always tried to pose straight on for photos and I spent more time in the mirror putting on eye makeup, pretending there was no nose to study at all.

I confessed to my husband, many years after high school, that I couldn't stand my nose. I'd never admitted it to anyone before; to speak these words was to make them irrevocably true. I was afraid that maybe he'd never noticed it before. If I drew attention to it, would he ever stop noticing?

"I just want a different nose," I said, relieved to have it out in the open.

"Why?" He blinked, taken aback. "I like your nose."

"You do? Why? What's to like about my nose?"

"It suits you," he said, shrugging. "It was my favorite part about you when we were younger. And now it's even better."

"How?" I was nearly dumbfounded by this information.

"Well," he began, using a tone I had come to know as *treading lightly*. "You just needed to grow into it. Your nose is distinctive and when you were younger, it was out of proportion to your face. Now, you've grown into it."

The revelation gave me chills, but most definitely not in the way he intended. I knew he meant the words kindly, that he honestly liked my nose and wanted me to see it that way too. What he didn't realize was the depth of my hatred for this singular body part, and that telling me *it suits me* and *I grew into it* could only mean one thing: I was now as ugly as my nose. It had won. I was doomed.

So, it has been for a long time: living with the enemy, trying not to be ashamed to take photographs, and praying that my two children will not inherit my nose. It stopped taking over my life and became a constant din in the background of my self-image. I learned to focus on the things that I liked about my appearance, but I always knew I could never truly love myself until I accepted every part of me as special and beautiful. It felt like a lost cause.

Everything changed in the most unexpected of ways, however, when I was 30 years old and cradling my newborn son. The phone rang that night around 11 p.m. It was my mother, with the news I had been dreading.

"Mama's gone, Stephie," she whispered, barely able to say the words. My grandmother, my Mama, had lost an eight-year battle with Alzheimer's. I had known it was coming, had gotten all the updates daily about her deteriorating condition, but was unable to travel the 500 miles to be with her due to my recent Caesarean surgery.

The pain and grief, combined with the restrictions from my doctor that kept me in Massachusetts and not in New York with my family, spurred me to memorialize her in any way I could. I gathered all the photos I had of her: bringing me to the playground, holding me as an infant, feeding me my first mashed potatoes. I had some older pictures of her as well, pictures of her getting married and holding her own children for the first time. Some were even pictures of my grandmother when she was about 30 years old too. She was beautiful and she had always been my hero, and I was left to mourn her loss alone and so very far away.

Then one day, it finally happened. I woke up, brushed my teeth, and glanced in the mirror to check how bad my bed-head looked that morning. As my eyes scanned my face, they stopped on one feature they were very familiar with: my nose. I gasped, studying it in a brand-new way. It was hers, my grandmother's. It was also mine, my very own nose. In all of those pictures, it had been so very beautiful on her and now on my face, it stood as a gift from her to me.

My nose had never looked quite so special before.

I CAN'T BELIEVE I SAID THAT...

When you're a kid, it's horrifying to think that you will grow up to say the phrases that all parents say. "You sound like your mom" is a terrible thing to be told, especially by your peers. The fact that I just used the word "peers" is one of those things that I can't believe I would even say.

Old people say "peers." Ugh.

Anyway, any parent can tell you that the trap is set long before we have children. The phrases are there, just waiting for that moment when you have nothing left to say. That little part of your memory has been clutching to these phrases since your youth. They are loaded up into the cannon, waiting for you to light the fuse. Your child is nagging you, asking why, why, why. He can't understand why you keep saying no. You know he won't understand the long answer. And so, you light the match and hold it beneath the fuse of the cannon. The next thing you know, you actually say these words out loud:

"Because I said so!"

And there it is. Your worst nightmare has come to pass.

MY LIFE IN YOGA PANTS

You are now one of THOSE parents. You took the easy way out, you forewent your ability to stand strong in the face of adversity. You are ashamed.

I've lived it, too. I'm not proud. I still can't believe I said it. Phrases like these are predictable and make you feel really uncreative. Luckily for all of us, children are pretty inventive little people and that means there will be scenarios you are not already armed to combat. Yes, it's true.

Sometimes when I say, "I can't believe I said that," it is not because I sound like my parents. Instead, it is because I sound absolutely ridiculous. These are the things my husband and I talk about later, after the kids are in bed and it is safe to laugh at ourselves. I can't believe I NEEDED to say these things, really.

And so, we have begun compiling a list of these unbelievable words of caution. These are all real words that have actually been said by me or my husband to one (or both) of our children. Here they are, in no particular order.

1. Please don't lick other people's cars.
2. No. Yogurt is not for painting.
3. We don't bite other people's butts.
4. Stop wiping your boogers on the dog.
5. It's not okay to pull on someone's eyelids.
6. People can't eat dog food.
7. No yoga on the stairs!
8. Nope, nope. Please don't stick your hands in your pants to touch the poop.
9. You cannot put a leash on your brother.

10. Duct tape is NOT for mouths!

For my children's sakes, I really hope these phrases are not the ones they remember us saying. I'm okay with them looking back and laughing about phrases like "I don't care who started it, I'm finishing it" or "Keep your hands to yourselves!" These are fine. They are safe. They are multipurpose. There are so many reasons these phrases still hang around.

While staircase yoga will always be frowned upon, I really just don't think it's got staying power for a future generation. I can't believe I've said these things and I really hope I don't need to again.

CAFFEINE FREE: A SHORT STORY

You wake up, disoriented for a moment, before you can identify which of the baby monitors is the source of this particular scream. You head left for the boy's room, where you fumble around in the predawn light peeking in between the blinds to find him in his crib, locate a clean diaper and mix a fresh bottle. It's no longer necessary for you to see well to be successful, nor is it important for you to be fully conscious; your auto-pilot parent is on cruise control all night long, meaning that a tiny part of you never actually gets to sleep. You don't think about this now, though, because you must place your ten-month-old back in the crib with his bottle and stumble across the hallway to check on your first born, the three-year-old girl with the curly hair.

    She is sleeping soundly, albeit it at strange angles that you would be positive weren't possible for human joints to create if you hadn't seen the proof with your own eyes. Two of her small limbs are hanging over the edge of the bed, free of the covers, and she has started to slide off the mattress.

You adjust her, careful not to wake her up, and tuck her back into the covers in a much more natural position for her little body. For a second, you admire her sleeping form in the light of her Mickey Mouse nightlight. If only she were so peaceful in the light of day.

Back in your own room, you glance at the clock, nearing 5 AM, and briefly entertain the notion that you could shower, do an entire yoga workout, and maybe drink a full cup of coffee before your tiny monsters arise for the day. The call of bed and the peaceful sounds of your husband's slumber, however, are too much for you to resist. It's warm and snug there, and you were having such a good dream.

Next time you wake, it's because of an alarm that's screaming and the movement of your husband leaving the warm cocoon of your duvet. You know you should shower and dress, but only one eyelid manages to open. Maybe just a few more moments and then you'll—the monitor sounds. The little people who need you are stirring, waking up for the day, getting restless in their beds. No shower, no coffee...today is already off its axis. Your feet haven't even touched the ground yet.

The next eight hours of your husband's work day pass in a blur. You change diapers, toss pajamas into the hamper, wrestle tiny arms and legs into fresh clothes, haul both children downstairs, find PBS on the television, wipe down a high chair, locate a booster seat, and turn on the Keurig. You manage to find a clean coffee cup and press Brew, but walk away when a scream draws you back into the dining room, where cereal has been thrown and now coats the carpet beneath the table. You clean it, replace it, and then supervise that this second bowl gets eaten. A new program comes on the TV and the toddler pitches a fit, so you dig the remote from the couch cushions and find a new channel. A bright pink bear dances on screen, singing a hypnotic song, and a hush falls over the room.

You sneak away to put creamer in your coffee, but find it has cooled. You stick it in the microwave for forty-five seconds and then dart downstairs to grab the laundry from the drier so you can find a clean pair of yoga pants to wear for the day. You dress downstairs, straining to hear any noises from your two hypnotized children, then rush back to release them from their chairs just as they begin to throw things again. You relocate them to a child-proof space. Within minutes of entering the play area in your living room, your children have emptied every toy from the bins and covered the floor with tripping hazards. But you leave them alone, because they're quiet and you still haven't had any—Coffee! You check; it's gone cold already. You slam the door of the microwave closed and punch in the numbers again.

Another scream emanates from the living room, this time from your son. You assess the situation, return the toy his sister stole to his sticky little hands, and glance at the clock. Time for school!

You change diapers again, throw a box of raisins into your daughter's backpack for snack time, and wrestle tiny arms and legs once again, this time into car seats. You're not wearing shoes, however, so you dart back in the house for a pair of shoes—any shoes—and reemerge with two different-colored flip-flops. It's only October, it could still be flip-flop season somewhere. But you're not worried about that and you drive off.

You drop your daughter at preschool and then rush through your circuit of weekly errands. You return books at the library, picking out two new titles—one on potty training for your stubborn daughter and one about a monster who picks his nose and has no friends because of it. You deposit checks at the bank ATM, the one that is set back too far from the road so you have to open your car door and lean through the open window to reach the buttons. You slip while doing this and lose a flip-flop. Dammit! The car behind you beeps, but you're not leaving without your footwear.

Shoes on, you head to the grocery store and realize you left the list on the refrigerator. And the bottles you were going to redeem. You try to remember what you needed to get, ask the baby—who just gurgles and smiles at you—and decide to walk up and down every aisle to try to jog your memory. Instead, you forget to buy milk and eggs and end up with Oreos, a pack of Twizzlers, and a no-name box of Twinkie knock-offs. You swear you have no idea where these things came from.

By the time you pick up your daughter from school, the cold groceries are nearly melted and you have to speed back to the house. A cop passes you and your heart stops, but you don't get pulled over. You do, however, hit a squirrel who darts out in front of your tires, mourn the loss of this tiny rodent over the phone with animal control, and get home so late that the cold groceries are now lukewarm.

At least you forgot to buy that milk.

Your husband pulls back into the driveway just as you finish unloading the last bag of groceries. It's time to toss the kids in the bath and get dinner started and he says he will help. And just as you strip down the kids for their baths, wrestling tiny arms and legs out of clothes this time, your husband shouts up from the kitchen: "Hey, did you know you left a coffee in the microwave?"

ABOUT THE AUTHOR

Stephanie Haddad is usually a fiction writer. Her titles include *A Previous Engagement, Love Regifted, Love Unlisted, Socially Awkward,* and *Under Renovation.* She has also published a collection of short stories, *Other Kinds of Love,* and is hard at work on a follow-up essay collection titled *My Life in Travel Mugs.* She's come a long way from her first stories about pumpkins and unicorns, but she still believes in happy endings. Stephanie lives north of Boston with her loving husband, daughter, son, and their unflappably happy dog, Max.

Visit www.stephaniehaddad.com for more information on upcoming titles and other news.

Made in United States
North Haven, CT
16 September 2022